THIS BOOK BELONGS TO

I LOVE TO
fart

YES, I
FART
BUT MY
MOM
STILL LOVES ME

I JUST FARTED
SO SUPER HARD

I CAN TASTE
YOUR FARTS

I'M NUTTER THAN A
SQUIRREL
FART

WARNING!
HORSES MAY BITE, KICK & FART!

FACT: Sometimes when a dragon farts, a little fire comes out.

I BET GIRAFFES DON'T EVEN KNOW WHAT FARTS SMELL LIKE

THE FART OF SILENCE

DO YO HEAR
WHAT I
HEAR ?

OK GUYS
WHO'S GOT A
LIGHTER

NEVER TRUST
A FART

I NEED TO
FART

FARTING
EVEN DUCKS
DO IT

FLUFFY & SWEET
FLAMINGO
FARTS

I DON'T
EAT
ANYTHING
THAT
FARTS

www.ingramcontent.com/pod-product-compliance
Lightning Source LLC
LaVergne TN
LVHW080822141224
799120LV00015B/1524
9798733615288